WATERCOLOUR PAINTING

with Aubrey Phillips

WATERCOLOUR PAINTING

with Aubrey Phillips

B.T. Batsford Ltd, London

Dedication
This book is dedicated to my darling
Bee because without her help it would
never have been finished.

First published 1997

ISBN 0 7134 7080 1

A catalogue record for this book is available
from the British Library.

Published by
B.T. Batsford Ltd
583 Fulham Road
London SW6 5BY

Printed in Hong Kong

CONTENTS

INTRODUCTION

The medium of watercolour has continued to exercise a fascination over me since as a young student I first experienced its discipline. Watercolour has a character of its own which sets it apart from any other medium and makes it well suited to capturing changing light and weather conditions. By its very nature, its transparency, it seems essentially a medium for evanescent atmospheric effects. The way in which washes float into each other can suggest a lazy drift of cloud softening the shape of mountains and veiling the distant landscape in mystery. What an inspiration it is, and what an uplifting experience, to study the works of the great masters of the past and the traditions they have bequeathed to us. Turner with his 'Golden Visions', John Sell Cotman, David Cox, John Constable, Thomas Girtin, Peter de Wint and others – each with their own individual style contributing to that Golden Age which blossomed at the end of the eighteenth and beginning of the nineteenth centuries.

Previous to this, watercolour was not recognized as a medium of any great significance. Albrecht Dürer (1471–1528) produced some notable watercolour landscapes and watercolour was later used to illustrate famous personages' travels on their Grand Tour of Europe. Today we can rejoice in the fact that it is afforded equal status with other mediums. I do urge the reader to study early paintings, for we can learn so much from them and they are readily available to us in many galleries around the world.

We are naturally drawn more to the work of some painters than others and it is likely that they will influence our own work to a

Figure 1 *Mawddach Estuary*. 55 x 42 cm (22 x 16½ in.).

Figure 2 *Reflections*. 29 x 36 cm (11½ x 14 in.), charcoal study.

certain extent. Painters have always been influenced from the dawn of civilization and this has led to the development of the great schools and movements which have contributed so much to our culture. We all have personal feelings and tastes, which is as it should be. I am personally drawn to the direct use of watercolour for there is, I feel, a beauty in a wash of watercolour with the light of the paper showing through, quite apart from what it may convey as a picture. There is a general tendency today to include in watercolour exhibitions opaque work which is classified as water-based, but for me the true essence of watercolour is its transparent nature – pure washes obtained without any use of body colour, masking fluid, wax resistants, texturing materials or other foreign bodies.

Drawing

I consider drawing to be the foundation of painting in any medium, but this does not necessarily mean that drawing is restricted to the use of pencil or pen. In drawing we create the feeling of form, volume, weight, texture, etc., which in painting is often conveyed by the brush. This can be done in a variety of ways; for example, some of the Impressionists used patterns of dots of pigment to build up form in a technique called pointillism.

This book contains several illustrations of my charcoal sketches, which I make in preparation for painting. In these I can study the problems of composition, tone and drawing, and the shapes, volume and texture of my subject matter. I try to see one shape against other shapes – for example the shapes of mountains against the background of the sky, white and grey cloud shapes against a blue sky, trees against mountains, buildings against trees, and so forth. Initially I assess the shapes in the simplest terms possible within this relationship, and then I begin to develop such detail as I find necessary upon this foundation.

Although there are no lines in nature, the use of line in drawing is a symbol which we can accept and pens, pencils and other such instruments are normally used for this purpose. There is plenty of expressive and sensitive work produced in this way, but it is nevertheless advisable to be aware of the various other methods of expression that are open to us to explore.

Many of the pictures illustrated in this book were painted direct, building up the drawing, particularly in the latter stages, with only the aid of the brush. In my early days I felt the need of a drawing over which to paint but now I have the confidence and experience to work directly with the brush. It is, of course, sound technique to draw initially with pencil or pen and to wash over this, retaining the drawing as part of the finished work if desired, although in certain soft passages a line showing through could be detrimental. There are certain instances where linework can be helpful in a painting, such as when dealing with a clearly defined building or similar important feature. I find the use of black Indian ink plays a dominant part in providing added strength.

CHAPTER 1
Tools and Materials

There is a bewildering array of brushes, paints and other materials on the market, and a beginner may feel confused when confronted with them all. Start simply with a few brushes and a small palette. You will soon learn how to mix colours and apply the paints to the different surfaces.

Brushes

I try to use as large a brush as possible in all my work. My largest and most often used is a no. 14 sable, plus smaller sable brushes nos. 11 and 8. Sable brushes are very expensive, being produced by skilled craftsmen, but they are well worth the cost. They last for years, retain their point and hold a wash well.

Figure 3 My raffia brush folder, paintbox and china saucers for preparing washes.

Good-quality nylon brushes are also available and I use a flat 2.5 cm (1 in.) brush for Indian ink, keeping my sables for pure watercolour. Great care must be taken to wash out all traces of Indian ink after use as it can dry hard and ruin a brush, so I prefer not to put my sable brushes at risk. I also use a nylon rigger brush, no. 4; this has long bristles which I use on the inside, dragging the brush over the paper to make use of the surface. Used on its point, a rigger is useful for drawing in detail such as tree branches, etc. It derives its name because it was originally used to draw in the fine lines of rigging in paintings of sailing ships.

A 7.5 cm (3 in.) brush is also part of my equipment. I find it of particular use in large-scale work, and for dealing with skies. I keep my brushes in a folder which I made from a raffia placemat, with strips of elastic threaded through at top and bottom to create loops which keep the brushes in position. I can put them away after working outside, rolling the mat up and tying it with the tapes which are attached. The brushes are then protected and can dry out naturally. It is not advisable to put wet brushes in a metal container which does not allow air to penetrate.

Drawing materials

I have a few soft pencils between 2B and 6B, a pure graphite 9B pencil, a charcoal 2B pencil and sticks of charcoal to use with a putty eraser for 'lifting out' when making studies. I find sticks of both black and white conté helpful, particularly when used together on tinted sugar paper.

I shape flat strips of balsa wood into working points to use with Indian ink (Figure 4). A hog's hair brush is useful for washing out and softening hard edges. I also use a couple of fibre-tip pens, one with a chisel end, the other pointed.

Figure 4   Strips of balsa wood can be shaped into various working points (as illustrated right) and used with Indian ink to form different types of mark.

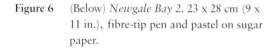

Figure 5 (Above) *Newgale Bay 1*. 23 x 28 cm (9 x 11 in.), soft pencil with written notes. Sketched from the car during rain.

Figure 7 (Above) *Newgale Bay 3*. 23 x 28 cm (9 x 11 in.), charcoal pencil. Sketched from the car during bad weather.

Figure 6 (Below) *Newgale Bay 2*. 23 x 28 cm (9 x 11 in.), fibre-tip pen and pastel on sugar paper.

Figure 8 This photograph shows how to use your watercolour paint in a diffused wash to create an effective sky.

Figure 10 I prefer to stand when I am working in the studio, with my drawing board set at an angle of about 30 degrees.

Figure 9 As you can see here, the angle at which the board is tilted allows the washes to flow freely down the paper, which is important as I flood them on in quite a liquid form.

Paints

I have a paintbox containing twelve pans, into which I add colours as required from the tubes. My paintbox contains mixing areas but I like to have at hand a few china saucers in which I can prepare large washes. Paints are available in student quality and artist quality. Artists' colours are richer in pure, finely ground, permanent pigments. They also tend to mix well and are transparent and luminous but, as you might expect, they are also more expensive than students' paints.

Figure 11 Try to set up all your equipment within easy reach. It is also helpful if there is a window in your studio as your paintings will benefit if you are able to work in natural light.

CHAPTER 2
Colour and Techniques

It is surprising that the use of colour was once seen as disreputable. Colour was of the senses, while form was the more superior function of the intellect. For centuries this belief formed a barrier to freedom of artistic expression until impressionism arrived at the end of the nineteenth century. We owe this artistic movement much of our pleasure today in looking at the world with an enlarged range of vision. Our eyes are open to the colour in shadows and we pause to look at a passing effect of light which otherwise would have gone unnoticed.

Landscape painters need the right range of colours to express what inspires them. My palette consists of the following colours:

Monestial Blue A greenish blue, good for skies and, mixed with Burnt Sienna or Burnt Umber, for dark greens.

French Ultramarine I use this colour widely, particularly for greys, mixed with Burnt Umber or Burnt Sienna.

Cobalt Blue This is useful in skies. Mix with Light Red for clouds or distant hills.

Burnt Sienna Warm and transparent; good for foregrounds, undergrowth and old bracken. Mix with Monestial Blue for strong dark greens for shadowed trees.

Burnt Umber Like Burnt Sienna, it gives darker tones. Mixed with French Ultramarine, it produces useful greys which can be adjusted to warm or cool.

Raw Umber Mixed with Viridian, it results in a good green.

Viridian Used in pale washes it gives cool greens for distant fields, etc.

Lemon Yellow Mix with Viridian and Raw Sienna for a light, sunny green.

Raw Sienna More transparent than Yellow Ochre. Mixed with Light Red, it can give warmth to clouds, sunlit buildings, etc.

Light Red Mixed with French Ultramarine or Cobalt Blue, makes light to mid-toned greys.

Cadmium Red Useful for bright touches of colour on boats.

Alizarin Crimson Useful mixed with French Ultramarine and Cobalt for purples and mauvey greys.

Blending colours together while they are still wet.

Monestial Blue
over Lemon Yellow

French Ultramarine
over Raw Sienna

Cobalt Blue
over Light Red

Alizarin
over Viridian

Washes over other dried washes reveal watercolour's transparency.

French Ultramarine
and Burnt Umber

Burnt Sienna
and Monestial Blue

Raw Sienna
and Viridian

Lemon Yellow,
Raw Sienna and Viridian

Light Red and
Raw Sienna

Light Red and
Cobalt Blue

Raw Umber and
Viridian

Cadmium Red and
Cobalt Blue

Alizarin and French
Ultramarine

Working outdoors

As a landscape painter it is very important to carry out as much of my work as possible direct from nature, where I can at least attempt to understand the various moods and seasons of the year.

Using watercolour outdoors can be difficult, and at times virtually impossible. On damp, misty days, washes dry very slowly or not at all. But it is often these conditions which present us with the type of subject ideally suited to watercolour.

In these circumstances, as you can see from the illustrations, I often make a study in charcoal, conté, biro or soft pencil, which I can use for reference later in the studio. There are occasions when the weather conditions make it impossible even to resort to these methods, so then I try to retain in my memory the essentials of the subject, enabling me to carry out a rough sketch when I return home which I can develop into a completed work later.

When conditions are suitable I often paint on a small scale, 19 x 28 cm (7½ x 11 in.), which allows me to work quickly. I usually begin by washing in the sky and

Figure 12 *Brecon Beacons*. 23 x 28 cm (9 x 11 in.), soft pencil and charcoal pencil with written notes. Sketched from the car when a strong, cold wind made working outside difficult.

Figure 13 *Falls on the Braan*. 23 x 28 cm (9 x 11 in.), fibre-tip pen. I was prepared to work out in the rain to capture this study and the tones blended together on the wet paper. I later produced a full-colour picture from this sketch.

other light areas on the first sheet of paper, leaving it to dry while I follow the same procedure on other sheets. I can then return to the first sketch, which has usually dried sufficiently to allow me to work on it, and continue with the others. The end result, looking at three or more studies, can be quite interesting, especially as in this way I may have been able to capture the changing mood of the scene.

I find a waterproof map container, as used by walkers, useful for carrying a small sketchbook. It has small pockets which can be used to hold pencils, small pieces of charcoal, eraser, conté, etc. The whole thing is very light and has a shoulder strap, so it can be used for very brief, quiet studies when other work is impossible.

I usually take a small folding stool to sit on and have my paintbox, water container and other equipment at my feet. Everything is contained in a rucksack which I can sling over my shoulder, allowing me to walk freely around. I do not usually find the need to carry an easel, although there may be times when a subject is better seen from a standing position. I always have one available in the car.

I often find winter subjects so inspiring that I am prepared to suffer a certain discomfort when sketching them. The sun is not as high in the sky, causing long shadows, and with the trees bare of foliage we can see subject matter which would not be visible in summer. A fall of snow can transform the landscape and cause a complete reversal of normal tonal relationships, with the snow often lighter than a stormy sky. I wear warm, windproof clothing (cold winds are the greatest problem) and sound footwear.

Exercises in wash techniques

In Figure 14, I created the waterfall study by mixing Monestial Blue with Burnt Sienna and, using the brush on its side, dragging it across the dry surface of the paper, adding a touch of Raw Sienna while it was still wet. I carried the same wash into the water area below, adding a touch of Burnt Umber to the bottom right and a little Burnt Sienna above. Finally the two rocks were put in with Burnt Umber and a little French Ultramarine, with a stronger wash of the same for the shadows when dry and a little Raw Sienna on each side. I took care to keep the dry paper untouched for the lights.

For the tree study I mixed Burnt Umber with Monestial Blue. Dragging the brush on its side over the dry paper suggested the texture of a winter tree. I drew in the trunks and branches with the point of the brush.

For the boats on the beach I washed in pale Monestial Blue for the sky, with Light Red (also pale) for the beach area below. With the sky wash beginning to dry, I drew in the distant headland to the right of the boats using Ultramarine and Burnt Umber with a slight tint of Monestial Blue for the sea to the left. I then washed over the beach area in a combination of these colours. The sky was now completely dry and against it I drew in the boats and figures, using a variable wash of Ultramarine and Burnt Sienna. Their reflections were suggested in the beach below, which was still damp.

For the seashore I again used a pale wash of Monestial Blue for the sky, adding a little Light Red and Ultramarine for the soft cloud. I continued the soft Monestial Blue over the sea area into pale Light Red and Raw Sienna for the beach. When dry, I shaped up the distant headland to the right with Ultramarine and Burnt Umber, using a darker tone with a little more Burnt Umber for the nearer cliffs to the right. Viridian and Lemon Yellow gave me the nearer light green area with a little Burnt Sienna for the darker part. The sea was darkened with Monestial Blue and Burnt Sienna, and the shadowed areas of beach with Light Red and a little Ultramarine. The small figures were drawn in on a dry background, with a little Cadmium Red for the ones on the left and the right, and Ultramarine and Burnt Umber for the centre figure. I was careful to leave untouched white paper for the foam at the edge of the sea.

Waterfall

Trees

Figure 14 Exercises in wash techniques.

Boats on the beach

Seashore

A: Stage 1

B: Stage 1

A: Stage 2

B: Stage 2

Figure 15 *Moorland Cottage*. Demonstrations A (left) and B (right) show the same subject treated with different wash techniques.

Moorland Cottage

The above illustrations show how a subject can be simply transformed with different wash techniques. Try some experiments yourself with different strengths of colour, laying both flat and more textured and dramatic washes.

Demonstration A: Stage 1

I painted the background wash of the sky with Monestial Blue at top left. Leaving areas of the paper uncovered for the lights, I added a little Light Red and Raw Sienna. I then added a stronger mixture of French Ultramarine and Burnt Umber for the dark clouds, using the same mixture lower down above a pale wash of Raw Sienna. These washes blended together, giving a soft effect which I allowed to dry.

Stage 2

I next mixed a wash of Ultramarine and Burnt Umber, darker than used previously, and washed in the shape of the distant hills while carefully drawing it round the form of the buildings. A darker tone of Burnt Umber and Ultramarine was drawn in at the base of the distant hills on each side of the buildings, and for the stone wall leading in from the left. The detail on the buildings was also drawn in with this mixture. A touch of Burnt Sienna gave the colour of the lower roof to the right, and a mid-toned wash of Burnt Umber provided a shadow across the foreground. The light tones of the buildings were the actual colours used in the sky, their forms having been created by carefully washing in the tones of the hills behind.

Demonstration B: Stage 1

I washed in the sky using the same colours as in Demonstration A, Stage 1, but with less cloud formation and with a light green foreground, using Lemon Yellow, Viridian and Raw Sienna. I allowed these to dry.

Stage 2

I then mixed up a strong tone of French Ultramarine with a little Burnt Umber and drew in the dark roofs and chimneys of the buildings, taking care to leave the light of the gables to the left, which I had already washed in and allowed to dry. Burnt Sienna was added for the lower roof to the right and a dark green using Viridian and Burnt Sienna was washed in at the base of the buildings and in the foreground.

Techniques

• Try sketching in different media – charcoal, conté, soft pencil or fibre tip.

• Memorize a subject and sketch it when you get home.

• Overcome adverse weather conditions by making studies on the spot to use as reference later in the studio.

• Working on a small scale allows you to work quickly and to work on more than one study at once.

• If you want to create points of light, remember not to wet the dry paper.

Working over ink drawing

The use of black Indian ink drawing gives added strength to a watercolour and provides texture. In such studies I experiment with various types of wood cut into convenient shapes, allowing me to make different marks, both lines and broad strokes (see Figure 4, page 11). Some types of soft wood, such as that used in lollipop sticks or strips of balsa wood, are suitable for this. Both are rather absorbent and retain the ink for a time, making it possible to achieve a soft, textured effect by drawing the stick in a partly dry state across the surface of the paper. The surface of the paper plays a very important part in this technique – I find the Not surface best. Washes of colour applied over these drawings can be very direct as the tone and textures have been established with the ink. The following example illustrates this technique.

Spring Sunshine

I first drew in the main shapes with a soft pencil and then applied the ink, using a piece of balsa wood shaped to a workable point.

The waterproof ink soon dried, allowing me to lay in the washes, beginning with the sky. I used Monestial Blue to the left, drifting in Raw Sienna and Light Red to the right, and a grey composed of Cobalt Blue and Light Red. I retained areas of dry paper to act as highlights. Before the sky was dry I washed in the distant hills, again with a mixture of Light Red and Cobalt Blue. This blended into the damp surface to give a soft, distant effect.

I next mixed Lemon Yellow, Viridian and Raw Sienna for the light, sunny green of the sunlit grass on the road verges on each side, with a pale wash of Viridian for the distant field behind the main tree.

Light Red and Cobalt Blue in a pale mixture was applied to the road and to the cart track below the main tree. I covered the buildings with a light wash of Raw Sienna. I washed in the same light green for the large tree and the smaller one to the right as I had used on the grass verges. The distant group of trees to the right of the house was a mixture of Monestial Blue and Burnt Sienna in a cool tone. I added a darker green to the large tree and the smaller one to the right, using Viridian and Burnt Sienna. I carried this down for the shadow from the large tree and the hedgerow on each side. Using a mixture of Cobalt Blue and Light Red, I washed in the tree shadow on the road and the darker tones on the buildings. Burnt Sienna provided the roof colours of the house and the low building to the right, with Monestial Blue for the roof of the other building near the house. The distant trees behind the large tree were drawn in with a cool blue-grey tint, using Monestial Blue and Burnt Sienna. This was carried over to the distant trees above the right-hand barn.

I was able to carry out this painting in a very direct way as the ink drawing had created the basic forms.

Figure 16 *Spring Sunshine*. 26 x 37 cm (10½ x 14½ in.), 440 gsm (200 lb) Bockingford paper. Textured ink drawing using balsa wood, overlaid with transparent washes.

Colour tips

• Choosing a range of colours including a warm and a cold shade of each primary plus some earth colours such as Raw Sienna will help you to capture the atmosphere of each landscape.

• Twelve colours form the basis of my palette and this range allows great flexibility (see pages 14-15).

• You can create further colour ranges by blending them while still wet.

Stormy Evening

It was an autumn evening in Sutherland and the sunset gave a dramatic background to the pounding waves as they shattered into the drifting spray against the rocks.

Working on the spot under such conditions was not possible so, after observing the scene for a time, I returned to base and made a charcoal study from which to work (Figure 17).

It was necessary to absorb as much as possible while I stood in the failing light because on turning away from the tumultuous water it would be all too easy to lose the spirit of the scene. I always find it best to begin work on such a picture as soon as I can, while the sight of the natural elements, whether the deep stillness of sunrise or a wind-torn coastline, is still fresh. In this case, while I began with a black and white sketch, recording the basic shapes of the coastline and the angry waves crashing on the rocks, I kept the colours of the scene uppermost in my mind all the time, in preparation for the first stage of painting.

Figure 17   Preliminary study for *Stormy Evening*. 29 x 42 cm (11½ x 16½ in.), charcoal.

Figure 18 *Stormy Evening.* Stage 1.

Stage 1

With a landscape like this, I begin by thinking about the materials I will use. I felt the heavyweight rag paper Richard de Bas would help me bring out the best of the scene, especially with so much white showing through!

I used a large sable brush and with my colours mixed I was away, sweeping big washes over the paper, watching with excitement how the paint receded from the raised surface, leaving behind the natural colour of the paper which can often enhance this kind of picture.

I washed in Light Red and Raw Sienna for the bright glow in the sky and drifted in Monestial Blue above and to the left. A mixture of French Ultramarine and Burnt Umber was used for the dark cloud to the right and also to the left of the bright area. A pale wash of Burnt Umber was carried across the lower foreground, taking care to preserve the paper untouched for the white breakers.

Figure 19 *Stormy Evening.* Stage 2.

Stage 2

I drifted in more of the Ultramarine and
Burnt Umber mixture behind the cliffs on the
right. When the paper had dried I shaped up
the cliffs, using a stronger grey of the same
mixture. Adding a little Monestial Blue,
I continued the cliff area below down
to the beach.

Figure 20 *Stormy Evening.* Stage 3.

Stage 3

A mixture of Monestial Blue and Burnt
Umber gave me the tone for the lower cliff
area to the right, and the rocks on the beach
over to the left. I continued the wash below
for the reflections in each case.

Stage 4: The finished painting

It was now time to add the final darks to the cliffs and rocks, creating a contrast to the light of the breakers. I also needed to give more definite form to the nearer areas against those farther back, which were made softer and less clearly defined by the drifting spray. I took care to retain most of the white of the paper here, but added a little Monestial Blue in a very pale wash for a translucent effect against the sky.

For the dark tones of the rocks, I used strong mixtures of Burnt Umber, Burnt Sienna, Monestial Blue and Ultramarine. I allowed them to blend together in certain passages, but kept them sharp in form against the spray and misty distance. For their reflections in the wet sands, I kept the edges soft by painting into a dark wash. When this area was dry, I dragged the brush over the surface to suggest the stones and seaweed on the sands.

Figure 21 *Stormy Evening*. Stage 4 (the finished painting), 28 x 38 cm (11 x 15 in.), 480 gsm (220 lb) Richard de Bas Rough paper.

Dartmoor Landscape

I find Dartmoor an attractive area for painting, with its wild rugged moorlands and windswept trees, which I have attempted to capture here.

I began with the sky, using Light Red and Raw Sienna for the warm clouds and adding a blue-grey, mixed with Light Red and French Ultramarine. When the sky was dry I washed in the distant hills with Ultramarine and Burnt Umber. I washed in the whole of the foreground area below the trees in Lemon Yellow, Viridian and Raw Sienna, with a few touches of Burnt Sienna dropped in while this was still wet to warm it up.

I then dealt with the trees, which were in dark silhouette against the sky, using a strong mixture of Monestial Blue and Burnt Sienna. I dragged the brush swiftly on its side over the surface of the paper to obtain the texture of the foliage and used its point to draw in the trunks and branches.

This same dark wash was repeated in the foreground together with a dark green, using Viridian and Burnt Sienna when this area was dry.

Figure 22 *Dartmoor Landscape.* 18 x 27 cm (7 x 10½ in.).

Figure 23 *Light over the Moelwyns.* 20 x 28 cm (8 x 11 in.).

Light over the Moelwyns

I painted this study on a high summer's day in North Wales. The impressive peaks of the Moelwyn Mountains were set against a sky of drifting clouds, which cast both light and shade on the landscape below.

I began with the sky, washing in a pale tone of Light Red and French Ultramarine. I left areas of the white paper for highlights and added a little Monestial Blue in the upper part. I then mixed up a darker tone of Light Red and Ultramarine for the darker clouds in the upper right area. I followed this with a pale wash of Raw Sienna over the whole of the foreground. When the sky was dry Ultramarine and Burnt Umber was used for the mountain range, washed in quickly but carefully to establish their impressive shapes against the light sky. Monestial Blue and Burnt Sienna gave the darker tones of the trees and shadows in the foreground.

View near Abergavenny

This study depicts a calm, still day in early
summer. I approached this subject in much
the same way as *Light over the Moelwyns*,
but with a brighter green foreground and the
distant houses giving a feeling of scale.

Green is one of the most commonly used
colours in landscape painting, but many
otherwise passable pictures are ruined by not
enough thought being given to the choice.
I prefer to create my own greens, using
mixes of Monestial, Cerulean and
Ultramarine Blue, Viridian, Yellow Ochre,
Raw Sienna, and/or Lemon Yellow. The
degree of yellow to blue will decide the
resulting green.

Techniques

- Keep the edges of your lines soft by painting into
  a wet wash when working with water effects or
  reflections.

- Give an impression of foliage by quickly dragging
  your brush on its side over the surface of the
  paper.

Figure 24 *View near Abergavenny.* 18 x 27 cm (7 x 10½ in.).

Cardigan Bay

For this atmospheric coastal scene, I washed in Raw Sienna with a little Light Red for the warm clouds and pale Monestial Blue for the background tints, taking care to leave large areas of the white paper for light. French Ultramarine and Burnt Umber were used for the headlands, with a pale wash in the distance drifting into the lower part of the sky, which was still wet, and a darker wash of the same mixture for the headland to the left. Monestial Blue and Burnt Sienna provided the colour of the sea and Burnt Umber in a light tint gave me the tone of the sands.

I preserved the white of the paper for the light waves. The figures added human interest and gave a feeling of scale.

The eye is always drawn to whatever has been chosen to set the scale so care must be taken deciding the placement of this important part of the composition. This is often a figure, but it could equally be a tree, building or boat.

Figure 25 *Cardigan Bay.* 18 x 27 cm (7 x 10½ in.).

Figure 26 *Cottage on Dartmoor.* 18 x 27 cm (7 x 10½ in.).

Cottage on Dartmoor

I felt that the dramatic stormy sky, partly covering the rugged shapes of the tors on the skyline, was in keeping with the wild Dartmoor atmosphere. The solitary cottage helped provide scale and interest in the greener area below, which contrasted with the stark contours above.

Techniques

- Figures in the landscape add human interest and a sense of scale.

- When adding shadows, take care to leave them more abstract in the distance and to develop more detail in the foreground.

- To give an impression of sunlight, lift off darker tones with a damp brush before they dry.

- Always allow the background to dry before painting any other elements, otherwise you will lose the definition of your work.

Figure 27 *May Morning.* 28 x 38 cm (11 x 15 in.), 300 gsm (140 lb) Saunders-Waterford paper.

May Morning

This scene was painted on a May morning with the mist clearing and the sunlight beginning to filter through. The distant part of the wood was soft and mysterious.

I began by using a light grey wash, using French Ultramarine and Burnt Umber in a very liquid state on dry paper. I added a light green mixture of Lemon Yellow, Viridian and Raw Sienna, continuing the combined wash (with the green

predominating in places) down to the foreground, where I began to add Monestial Blue in places and Ultramarine in others. I retained the white of the paper in parts to suggest the wood anemones and for the masses of bluebells.

I mixed Monestial Blue and Burnt Sienna for the darker green foliage, which I added to the upper parts of the trees while the paper was still damp, giving me the soft effect which was essential for the theme of the work. Using Ultramarine and Burnt Umber I added the softer, more distant tree trunks. As the paper began to dry I shaped up the nearer, darker tree trunks with Burnt Umber and Monestial Blue, together with the more clearly defined structure of the branches and darker foliage.

I then began to develop the foreground with warm areas of Burnt Sienna and Burnt Umber where old bracken showed among the grass, contrasting with the cool blue passages. I added the shadows cast by the trees, taking care not to make them too definite in the distance but developing more detail in the foreground. In order to express the effect of the sunlight on some of the tree trunks, I lifted off the darker tones (using a damp brush) before they were dry (see below).

Lifting off

In the two examples shown below, I have suggested light tree trunks and branches against a darker background. My procedure was to apply a wash and wait for it partly to dry. Using finger and thumb, I then squeezed the excess moisture from the brush, leaving it damp. Drawing the brush firmly over the paper surface, I lifted off the damp background, creating the light shapes of the tree trunks and branches.

It is important that the background is allowed to dry partly, otherwise a wet wash would immediately close over and cover any lighter shapes. Further shaping of the tree forms can be developed when the wash is dry. It is possible to wash off a dry surface using a hog's hair brush but this can damage the surface of the paper. I prefer to lift off as described as this creates soft edges.

Figure 28 Examples of lifting off watercolour to create the effect of light trees against a dark background.

CHAPTER 3
Perspective and Composition

Linear perspective

Although I don't consider it essential for a landscape painter to have a thorough knowledge of linear perspective, I do believe that at least a basic understanding of its principle is required. Perspective is governed by certain scientific facts and can be studied from the various reference books on the subject. It does not require any aesthetic feeling but it does help an artist to convey the sense of a third dimension on a two-dimensional surface.

The early Renaissance artist Ucello made considerable use of linear perspective in many of his works. In more recent times, the great J.M.W. Turner (1775–1851) was a supreme master in this subject and was for a period Professor of Perspective at the Royal Academy. Much of his early work consisted of architectural subject matter, in which he was able to use his knowledge of linear perspective. In many of his later works he seemed to cast aside this experience and instead concentrated on aerial perspective, probably more than any other painter before or since.

The principle of linear perspective is illustrated in Figure 29 where the lines of the buildings converge at eye-level in the distance, the figures also diminish in scale. Scale is another factor which can be used to convey the effect of objects receding into the distance. I have made use of this method in Figure 30: the nearest trees on the left are the largest while the other trees become smaller as they recede, as do the sizes of the fields. The laws governing linear perspective would, of course, still apply to the open landscape but less obviously.

Figure 29 An example of linear perspective – note how the figures diminish in scale.

Figure 30 Recession in scale in a landscape – the trees and fields become smaller
as they recede into the distance.

Oykel Bridge 6.4.80.

Figure 31 *Oykel Bridge*. 23 x 28 cm (9 x 11 in.), charcoal pencil. I attempted to establish the dark tones of the woods on each side of the track against the soft mountains in the distance. Note the receding telegraph posts which convey a sense of distance.

Students sometimes find it difficult to divide the view into distance, middle distance and foreground. Half closing the eyes helps to make important features stand out more clearly. This following paragraph on aerial perspective should be of help, but do make sure you know where the background ends and the middle of the painting begins (which in turn gives way to the foreground) before you start a painting.

Aerial perspective

This governs the changes in tone and colour values in objects receding into the distance, caused by the density of the atmosphere. Contrasts become muted, with colours tending towards blue and objects becoming less clearly defined. The atmosphere, as we know, changes with the weather – we see less clearly on a foggy day, while on a warm, sunny day we can see far into the distance. The atmosphere varies from one part of the world to another, for example in Mediterranean countries the atmosphere is cleaner than it is farther north.

Landscape painters can make full use of aerial perspective to create depth and recession in their work. It is significant, in this context, to compare the work of Italian artists with that of the Impressionists in France. The fickle climate and damp atmosphere of Britain greatly influenced the work of the watercolour school active during the latter part of the eighteenth and early nineteenth centuries.

At one time, when most artists worked indoors at large easels, the concept of aerial perspective was not really considered. When painting a portrait or a group, Velázquez or Gainsborough did not have to take into account the weather conditions outside nor how a landscape might recede into a misty background. With a commissioned family portrait, for example, the artist would just paint what was immediately in front of him.

It was only when the Impressionists began painting *en plein air* that the exciting discovery of aerial perspective was made. Of course this type of painting also brought about a much greater respect for watercolour which had not previously enjoyed the popularity of oils.

Somerset Maughan said that before he began a book he would 'walk around the subject for two years'. Artists generally cannot wait so long, as opportunities to paint a particular scene in the best light, weather and seasonal conditions often only happens once.

Once the decision has been made to begin I work for a while on the composition. This does not eliminate the need for adjustments later down the line. A tree may need to be modified perhaps because it dominates a particular area or because the composition is complete without it. Such matters have to be dealt with as the painting develops and sometimes this means a completely new start!

Composition

Composition is the foundation upon which a painting is built, whatever the medium. It is my first consideration when I am looking for and planning any work. Nature does not provide us with ready-made subjects; landscape painting would be very dull if it did. We need to create from the richness of the raw materials which are presented to us. Considering these matters is time well spent. To view a subject properly, you need to walk round it and observe it from different viewpoints. You will feel the need to emphasize certain elements at the expense of others according to your intention and taste.

A1

A2

B1

B2

Figure 32 Examples of weak and successful compositions.

Composition Sketches

This series of four simple sketches shows what to look for in a strong composition. It is always helpful to make preliminary sketches like these before you start to paint.

A1

This illustrates a weak composition. The full weight of tone and interest is on the left and the lines of the hills, clouds and roadway, all lead the eye out to the right.

A2

This is a more successful arrangement. The contour of the hills and the roadway lead the eye to the chief points of interest, the building and the tree to the left of it.

B1

This example shows too formal an arrangement. The eye-level runs right through the centre of the composition and the main tree, and its reflection, is centrally placed. The two smaller trees are equally sized and too regularly placed. All the weight is on the left, leaving an empty area to the right; the river also leads out to the right.

B2

This composition is better. The eye-level is set higher, giving a larger area of the river so that greater use can be made of the reflections, which form an interesting foreground. The riverbanks lead the eye into the distance, while the smaller trees on either side of the large tree are placed irregularly and get smaller as they recede.

Valley Farm

I was attracted to this farm nestling in the valley as if seeking the protection of the surrounding mountains. It made a good composition with the stream leading in from the foreground and the mountains sweeping down to enfold it. The farm buildings, being placed in the middle distance, were rather small in scale and therefore imparted a feeling of bulk and grandeur to the mountains towering above them. The warm colour of the barn and the tints at the base of the mountain on the left are a useful contrast to the darker and cooler tones of the mountains. A little of this warmth is echoed in the upper part of the sky. The sunlit passage across the middle distance plays a vital part, contrasting with the deeper tones above.

Figure 33 *Valley Farm*. 27 x 36 cm (10½ x 14 in.).

Landscape near Lake Bala

This picture has a more open aspect than *Valley Farm*. The mountains are set beneath an atmospheric sky which obscures part of the distance and creates a light area behind the trees to the left. The small buildings are light against the background of the mountains and, being small in scale, help give the sense of receding into the distance. The trees on the left provide a tonal balance to the dark mountains on the right, leaving a light area which allows the eye to pass through to the sky. The foreground has been kept simple to avoid any distraction from more interesting images above.

Figure 34 *Landscape near Lake Bala.* 26 x 37 cm (10½ x 14½ in.).

HUBREY R. PHILLIPS

Mountain Farm

Here the farm buildings provide scale and also a light tonal contrast against the darker mountains behind. A farm track with stone walls on each side leads the eye in to the trees on the right and then to the light buildings. The trees on the left balance those on the right. The sharp contours of the mountains are obscured by the drifting cloud on the right, without which the mountains would have been a hard continuous line lacking in atmosphere. The light and dark tones in the sky relate to the landscape below.

Perspective and Composition

- A basic understanding of linear perspective is always useful, even when working with organic shapes in the landscape.

- Use aerial perspective to give depth and recession to your landscapes.

- The actual positions of landscape features can be adjusted slightly in your painting to create a better composition.

- Look at the movement within your proposed composition to ensure the pleasing balance of lines, focal points and perspective.

- A dramatic contrast in scale can give immense strength to a landscape.

Figure 35 *Mountain Farm*. 35 x 53 cm (14 x 21 in.).

Demonstration: Summer Landscape

This subject is a fine example of aerial perspective. Tone and colour become softer and cooler as the objects in the landscape recede into the distance.

As in many of my paintings, the sky plays an important part in the composition and this picture was no exception. It was a fine, sunny day with a breeze drifting large clouds across the sky, creating areas of light and shadow on the landscape below.

Figure 36 *Summer Landscape*. Stage 1.

Stage 1

I washed in a warm mixture of Light Red and Raw Sienna for the warm cloud at top left, repeating this with a few touches lower down to the right. I then washed a pale tint of Monestial Blue in the top right area, allowing it to drift into the first wash in places which produced a soft effect. At the same time I was careful to retain areas of white paper for highlights. The paper being dry when I began work allowed me to do this. For the darker areas of grey cloud I added French Ultramarine with Burnt Umber and blended the combined wash, softening it at the base.

Figure 37 *Summer Landscape*. Stage 2.

Stage 2

The lower area of sky at the bottom right with the Ultramarine and Burnt Umber wash was still damp, so I mixed up a stronger mixture of the same colours. When this was applied, the mix of paint drifted in to give a soft effect. The other part was dry, so I carefully washed in the distant contours of the hills with a lighter wash of the same colours which dried with a clearly defined edge. These grey tones were then blended into a warmer wash of Raw Sienna with a little Burnt Sienna added. The wash was then carried down over the remainder of the paper, and allowed to dry.

Figure 38 *Summer Landscape*. Stage 3 (the finished painting), 29 x 39 cm (11½ x 15½ in.).

Stage 3: The finished painting

I next washed in the hills in the middle distance, again using Ultramarine with Burnt Umber; they were made gradually darker towards the foreground. I washed in Viridian in the middle distance to the left, blending it into Lemon Yellow and Raw Sienna. I was careful to retain this light passage as I drew in the darker tones. I then dealt with the near group of trees on the left, using Viridian with Raw Sienna for the lighter areas and Monestial Blue and Burnt Sienna for the darker, repeating these colours for the balancing group on the right. For the cool, strong tones of shadow on the middle-distance trees behind them, I used Ultramarine with Burnt Umber. To complete the picture I dealt with the foreground of corn stubble and straw bales, using a mid-toned wash of Burnt Umber with a little Raw Sienna. I tried to keep this as simple as possible, using texture and cultivation lines to lead the eye in.

Figure 39 *View near Lake Bala*. 28 x 37 cm (11 x 14½ in.).

View near Lake Bala

This painting shows a good example of aerial perspective. The nearest tree on the left is the darkest and warmest, with the wooded area beyond becoming slightly lighter and cooler, as are the smaller trees on the right. The mountains become gradually lighter and cooler in tone as they recede into the distance. I used warm greens in the foreground to help the receding effect. The soft grey mountain tones are reflected in the sky. This was a lovely day of moving light and shade over a fine, open landscape.

Figure 40 *Mawddach Estuary*. 25 x 37 cm (10 x 14½ in.).

Mawddach Estuary

This study shows an open view of the estuary under a bright sky, which is reflected in the water and lights up the middle distance. The wooded slopes on each side recede into the distance, from dark tones to cooler light shades, contrasting with the warm tones of the foreground.

Milford Haven

It is often necessary to make a tonal sketch from which to work later. Weather and light conditions and even the tide if you are working on a seascape will influence how long can be spent, but enough factual matter must go in to record the important features of the view. At Milford Haven I was anxious to portray the beach as a calm place where children played safely, quietly watched over by brooding cliffs. When the final picture is complete, the spirit of the original scene must shine through, giving the viewer an immediate sense of what drew you to it.

Figure 41 *Milford Haven*. 23 x 25 cm (9 x 11 in.), charcoal pencil. A tonal study using figures for scale, in preparation for a colour picture.

CHAPTER 4
The Artist's Eye

The eyes of an artist record the same images as those of any other person but it is the way in which we react to what we see that is important. Looking across an open field, for instance, a farmer would most likely consider how many sheep or cattle he could graze there. A speculative builder would probably calculate how many houses he could cram on to it. But an artist would gaze at the play of light and shade over the green grass and the reflected light from the sky, particularly if it was wet. Sadly there is another type of person to whom their eyes are only of use in preventing them walking into something. I often hear my students say how their eyes have been opened and how much natural beauty they have become aware of since they started to paint.

Each season offers new opportunities for the artist – spring with its pale new delicate foliage, summer with its rich vibrant greens, and autumn bursting with intense yellows,

reds and oranges. Perhaps for many people winter is not their favourite time of the year but I find it inspiring. I love the stark trees with their bare branches against a stormy sky, and to be able to look through their open framework to views which in summer would be obscured by foliage. Several winter scenes are illustrated throughout this chapter.

Stark Winter

I was attracted to this subject by the dark forms of the trees. Although not entirely bereft of their autumn foliage, they made a strong tone against the stormy sky. Their warm tints, together with the hedgerow below, created an attractive contrast to the cooler tones of the wooded distance. The patch of blue sky to the left is reflected in the rutted, snow-covered foreground.

Figure 42 *Stark Winter.* 29 x 39 cm (11½ x 15½ in.).

Ben Loyal

My eyes were certainly opened in my first view of this, my favourite mountain. Storm clouds covered the sky that day until the sun began to break through, gradually dispersing the curtain to reveal peak after shapely peak, rearing high above where only dark cloud had been before.

Ben Loyal presides over the gleaming waters and golden sands of the Kyle of Tongue like some protecting giant. I have tried to capture some of its beauty in this picture, on a bright day of moving light and shade.

I began to paint this picture by washing in the sky. Monestial Blue predominated to the upper right, with Light Red and Raw Sienna mixed for the light clouds and French Ultramarine and Burnt Umber for their shadowed undersides. Working quickly, I dragged the brush on its side to make use of the dry rough surface of the paper to retain areas of white and suggest moving clouds. Blending all these colours together, I brought them to the level of the water, repeating them in the foreground area of sand and water. I added Burnt Sienna to the Monestial Blue for the more distant level of water to the right, and left short accents of white paper. I drifted in Lemon Yellow, Viridian and Raw Sienna for the light green on the left-hand slope of ground. This completed what was, in fact, a continuous fairly light wash with the colours more or less drifting together. When the whole of the paper was dry, I carefully washed in the silhouette of the mountain against the sky with Ultramarine and Burnt Umber, and concentrated on drawing the rugged shapes. I needed to apply this quickly in one continuous wash before it could dry out and to bring it down to the distant waterline while avoiding taking it over the sloping green hillside on the left. While I was waiting for this to dry, I shaped up the darker passages of sand in the foreground with Burnt Umber. I then returned to the lower areas of mountain below the peaks, applying a wash of Ultramarine and Burnt Umber, a little darker than the previous wash, particularly to the left. Finally, using the same mixture, I shaped up the sloping ground to the left and applied a darker green with a Burnt Sienna/Monestial Blue mixture.

Figure 43 *Ben Loyal*. 26 x 36 cm (11½ x 15½ in.), 480 gsm.

Winter on the Windrush

There was a starkness in the bare trees to the left against the soft mists rising from the river. They were balanced by the distant trees on the right and the dark, warm tones of the foreground, contrasting with the cooler distance which formed a strong tonal base to the composition.

Artists are constantly reminding themselves to look and look again at the subject. Only by keeping to this strict discipline will he or she be able to make the necessary observations and mental notes which are so essential if the picture has to be finished later. Ask yourself exactly where does the mist give way, allowing a barn or figure to emerge or how can you can best capture the delicate new foliage of a group of trees in spring. Such observations must be imprinted on your memory to ensure the success of the final picture.

Figure 44 *Winter on the Windrush*. 29 x 39 cm (11½ x 15½ in.).

A Winter Stream

This was a raw, cold day in January, which would generally be considered by most people to be better spent at home in warm comfort. When there is a fall of snow I love to go out and look at it, even if I cannot do much about painting it on the spot. This was such an occasion. The calm (usual after a fall of snow) was emphasized by the still water of the stream. There was a warm glow in the late afternoon sky, which was echoed in the banks of the stream and the trees against the soft grey cloud behind. I took a good, long look to retain the image in my memory and painted it on my return in the comfort and convenience of the studio.

Figure 45 *A Winter Stream.* 28 x 38 cm (11 x 15 in.).

Figure 46 *Cumbrian Winter.* 25 x 35 cm (10 x 14 in.).

Cumbrian Winter

This was a keen, frosty evening with a stillness in the atmosphere which I wanted to convey in my painting. The grey strata clouds low in the sky made a contrast behind the distant snowy mountains, emphasizing their sharp peaks. The nearer mountains and woods were a dark, cool grey, while others were warm in contrast. The small buildings created a focal point, provided scale and suggested a human presence in what would otherwise have been rather a brooding scene. The whole subject composed well, with the stone wall in the foreground and the ruts in the snow leading the eye in to the picture.

Figure 47   *Study for Cumbrian Winter.* 25 x 35 cm (10 x 14 in.), charcoal.

The subtle tints in the sky were reflected in the snow-covered foreground.

I made a swift charcoal study to work out the composition and capture the basic shapes and contrasts in light and dark tones, so that I could translate it later in comfort.

When painting winter scenes, remember that snow is rarely white. Colour from the sky and clouds is reflected in beautiful pinks, greys and blues, while buildings and trees cast dark shadows across the surface, giving depth and atmosphere.

Techniques

- Warm tints combined with cooler tones will give effective contrast to a painting.

- Small buildings in a painting will create a focal point and a contrast in scale, as well as suggesting a human dimension.

Figures on the Beach

This was a simple subject with, at first glance, very little content. In direct contrast to the earlier bleak winter subjects, this was a warm, sunny day on the beach. I was attracted by the large clouds drifting across the sky. Their reflections in the sand, left wet by the receding tide, contrasted with the slightly darker dry areas of beach.

The figures gave scale and, with their reflections, provided a vertical element to contrast with the strong horizontal of the sea and dry sand.

Figure 48 *Figures on the Beach*. 28 x 38 cm (11 x 15 in.).

CHAPTER 5

Atmosphere, Sunlight and Shadow

It will be obvious from looking at the paintings in this book that atmosphere plays a very important part in my subject matter, as do sunlight and shadow. For me it is more essential to try to express effectively patterns of light and shade, the soft, almost magical, atmosphere of dawn and twilight, or the powerful and brooding quality of storm clouds about to break than to focus on minute detail. In the following pictures I will explain the ways in which I have dealt with these effects.

It would be misleading if I said that capturing atmosphere, sunlight and shadow is an easy matter for the artist. Even after a lifetime of painting it still exercises my mind more than any other aspect of my work. The word 'atmosphere' must be considered in two ways, firstly in terms of atmospheric perspective. Mist, hazy rain, fog or even dust can all affect atmospheric or aerial

perspective. There is another consideration, however, which is when atmosphere is being used in the sense of capturing the spirit or mood of a scene. Sometimes, when I am first drawn to a subject it seems to hold an indefinable quality – something so difficult to capture on paper but so worthwhile when rendered successfully. I always hope that the eventual owner of any such picture will discover this elusive quality and in so doing share in my enjoyment of it.

Figure 49   *A Cotswold Lane.* 33 x 48 cm (13 x 19 in.), 300 gsm (140 lb).

A Cotswold Lane

I have tried to capture the autumn sunlight in
the warm tints on the tall tree to the right
and the sunlit cottage bright against the
contrasting cool blue-greys behind. The
foreground is flooded in sunlight, the
shadows in the east contrasting with the light
road and verges.

Light over Jura

The light breaking through the clouds and reflecting on the water was my main reason for choosing to paint this subject. Everything else in the picture had to be in support of this theme. The grey clouds make a strong contrast against the light sky, blending their dark tones and veiling the peaks of the distant mountain on the right. The warm colours of the foreground were kept free of detail to provide a firm and simple base to the composition.

Sun and Rain Showers

The sun breaking through the clouds and lighting up the water on the coast of the Hebrides is similar in theme to *Light over Jura*. In this composition, however, it supports the detail and darker tones of the interesting croft in the foreground.

Figure 50 *Light over Jura*. 35 x 51 cm (14 x 20 in.).

Figure 51 *Sun and Rain Showers*. 29 x 39 cm (11½ x 15½ in.), 300 gsm (140 lb).

Figure 52 (Above) *Coniston Fells*. 25 x 37 cm (10 x 14½ in.).

Figure 53 (Right) *Glencoe*. 53 x 37 cm (21 x 14 in.).

Coniston Fells

The fading evening light behind the dark peaks, reflected in the still waters of the tarn, attracted me to this study. I kept the foreground low in tone and free from detail in contrast to the light water. The dark mountain peaks on the left make a strong contrast against the light sky. This was painted on a sheet of light grey paper, its natural tone retained in the light water of the tarn in the foreground.

Glencoe

The pass of Glencoe, steeped as it is in the history of clan warfare and with its high peaks often veiled in cloud, is charged with atmosphere. The drifting snow clouds softened the contours of the distant peaks, creating an atmosphere of mystery. The dark cool tones of the mountain in the middle distance gave a useful contrast to the light snow. The foreground rocks and water provide a strong horizontal base to the steep mountain slopes above.

Cast Shadows

In this study I attempted to capture the strong light behind the trees which cast their shadows over the rough surface of the foreground. I kept the foreground warm in colour and free of detail, and made use of the rough paper surface to suggest texture.

Bright Cloud

On this particular day the cloud was creating a strong top light which shone on the roofs of the buildings and cast shadows from the trees on either side. I kept the distance soft and misty in support of this theme and the foreground warm in colour and simple in treatment, with a little texture.

Figure 54   (Above) *Cast Shadows*. 57 x 24 cm (22 x 9½ in.).

Figure 55   (Right) *Bright Cloud*. 56 x 40 cm (18 x 15½ in.).

Farm Buildings

I wanted to capture the effect of the sun high above in the sky, top lighting the roofs of the buildings. I used the dark tones of the trees behind as a strong contrast. The dark, warm-toned hedgerow swinging in from the left takes the eye towards the buildings.

Let me remind students to carefully study the landscape and identify the distance, middle distance, and foreground.

This picture gave me scope to illustrate the recession of the hills, using muted colours, with the sun blending in softly against which the middle distance stands out. The farm buildings grouped below the hill hint at an extra quality of human interest. The composition of the picture as well as the effects of light, sunshine and shadows all contribute to the desired atmosphere.

Figure 56 *Farm Buildings.* 46 x 39 cm (18 x 15½ in.).

Figure 57 *Country Lane*. 36 x 44 cm (14 x 17½ in.).

Country Lane

I wanted to convey the shadows cast across the foreground of the picture from a strong light low on the left. I made use of the rough surface of the paper with a drier brush to give a broken light in the shadows.

A picture with buildings will often show little sign of life. Here, a human presence is suggested by the track leading to the farm.

Techniques

• Think about the interplay of light and shade. This will help you capture the atmosphere of a scene.

• Use a simplified tone of dark or light to emphasize a particular element in a painting.

Wet, Foggy Day

In foggy weather the moisture-laden atmosphere renders even close objects soft and vague, creating an air of mystery. I find this very attractive, especially when it is combined with reflections in the wet street.

A feeling of warmth and comfort is created by the welcoming lights in the building, contrasting with the damp discomfort of the figures down in the street.

Figure 58   *Wet, Foggy Day.* 26 x 30 cm (11½ x 10½ in.), charcoal.

Figure 59 *Evening Shadows*. 28 x 33 cm (11 x 13 in.), fibre-tip pen and charcoal.

Evening Shadows

This shows the evening light from the left, casting long shadows across the rutted, snow-covered foreground. The stark contrast between the dark silhouettes of the tree and shadows with the crisp light of the sky and the ground is a major feature of this piece.

The Harbour, Evening on the River, Crofter's Cottage

These three black-and-white studies all deal with evening light. I drew in the main forms using a broad-pointed fibre-tip pen, rubbed over with soft charcoal. The light areas were produced by lifting the charcoal off with an eraser. The charcoal can be freely applied and lifted off as required, leaving the pen drawing intact on the white cartridge paper.

Sometimes I feel restricting myself to black and white helps me to convey the essence of the scene without the distraction of colour. Painting this way can give a simple yet revealing impression of the qualities that drew me to the subject in the first instance.

Figure 60 *The Harbour.* 30 x 28 cm (12 x 11 in.), fibre-tip pen and charcoal.

Figure 61 *Evening on the River.* 28 x 36 cm (11 x 14 in.), fibre-tip pen and charcoal.

Figure 62 *Crofter's Cottage.* 29 x 38 cm (11½ x 15 in.), fibre-tip pen and charcoal.

CHAPTER 6
Weather and Mood

The effects of weather and mood play a more important part in my work than the mere rendering of cold topographical facts. I love to paint on a day of swiftly moving cloud, with the sun breaking through to create brilliant light alternating with deep shadows on the landscape below. Perhaps more surprisingly I particularly love winter. The rising mists from rivers or streams, when the forms of trees and buildings are veiled in mystery, have a far greater emotional appeal than when the same scene is viewed in a clear, flat light.

Winter on the Avon
This was certainly a mood subject, with the distant and mid-distant trees softened by the rising mists from the river. The sky had the look of more snow to come and, being dark, gave value to the light snow on either side of the river. I painted this picture in a fairly wet state throughout on Rough paper, which I retained untouched for the light snow.

Misty Evening
Beginning with the large area of sky, I added the distant trees while the sky was still wet in order to render the soft, misty atmosphere. The colours of the sky were repeated in the water. The nearer trees to the right and left were added when the paper was dry. I used warm, dark tones, dragging the brush on its side to produce the texture of twigs and the point of the brush for the trunks and branches. Warm tones were used in the reeds on either side of the stream.

Figure 63 *Winter on the Avon.* 29 x 39 cm (11½ x 15½ in.).

Figure 64 *Misty Evening.* 28 x 38 cm (11 x 15 in.), 440 gsm (22 lb) Bockingford paper.

Severn Estuary

I find estuaries particularly attractive
subjects. They compose better, with land on
each side, than an open coastline with land
on one side only and open sea on the other.
Here I attempted to capture the effect of
sunlight through the storm clouds and
reflecting on the distant water. The dark trees
on the left, together with their reflections,
form a useful contrast and are balanced by
the land on the right.

Perhaps my love of estuaries is due to the
feeling of tranquillity that often pervades.
Birds skim between the trees and over the
water while water-loving creatures make
their homes along the banks. Painting is pure
pleasure beside the quiet, almost still waters.

Figure 65 *Severn Estuary.* 36 x 53 cm (14 x 21 in.).

Figure 66 *Dovey Estuary.* 36 x 53 cm (14 x 21 in.).

Dovey Estuary

Showery weather was the main theme of this
picture. The sunlight was just beginning to
break through on the upper right, casting a
soft light over the sea. Everything was kept
soft, working into a damp background,
except for the dark forms of the boats on the
right and the sharp contour of the headland
on the left. These were painted in when the
background was dry. They balance each
other and contrast with the general soft
atmosphere.

Cardigan Bay

The warm glow of evening light sharpening
on the distant line of sea from behind a dark
storm cloud sets the mood of this study.
The shadowed sea contrasts with the light
horizon and the boats breaking through
provide a useful sense of scale.

Figure 67 *Cardigan Bay.* 51 x 36 cm (20 x 14 in.).

Cotswold Stream

The tall, stark trees on the left-hand side of the picture were very important in creating an upright element to contrast with the horizontal banks of the stream and features in the distance. I kept the sky light behind them so that, with its reflection in the water and the light of the snow, it provided a useful contrast. I used the warm tints of Light Red and Burnt Sienna in the foreground reeds on each bank, plus darker Burnt Umber tones. The latter contrasted with the cooler greys in the distance, comprising Burnt Umber and French Ultramarine. I was most careful to retain the white of the paper for the light snow and the reflections in the water.

Painting on Richard de Bas paper is pure luxury. It enormously enhances the painter's efforts in the way it accepts the paint from the brush, its creamy whiteness showing through in just the right places, creating touches of light in a naturalistic way.

Figure 68 *Cotswold Stream.* 29 x 38 cm (11½ x 15 in.), 300 gsm (140 lb) Richard de Bas Rough paper.

Figure 69 *Vale of Evesham*. 28 x 38 cm (11 x 15 in.).

Vale of Evesham

There was a soft atmosphere of evening light and a warm glow in the sky, with the distant Cotswold hills veiled in mist. The sky and the distance were worked in liquid washes, blending together, and the nearer darks were put in strongly when these washes were dry. The white of the paper was retained for snow, with Monestial Blue shadows contrasting with Burnt Sienna tones on the right.

In this beautiful part of England close to where I live, we are privileged in seeing some wonderful skies in winter. The way in which the muted colours including blues, pinks and greys are reflected on a snowy landscape is particularly inspiring.

Welsh Border

On a late winter afternoon, with the warm glow in the sky beginning to fade and the feeling of a cold night to come, I was walking around absorbing the general atmosphere, hoping to be able to capture it on my return to the warmth of the studio. I came upon a group of dark, warm-coloured trees in the hedgerow, creating a strong contrast against the light sky, balanced by some cooler-toned woods to the right. Frozen furrows lead the eye in from the foreground and the left-hand hedgerow leads into the distance. Everything combined to make a successful composition, so taking my sketchbook I made a quick charcoal study – an impression, together with a few written colour notes, sufficient to provide me with enough material to work from in the studio.

I began with the sky. It is rather overcast and makes a contrast with the white paper, which represents the snow. I washed in Light Red and Raw Sienna for the warm tints, particularly the right and lower parts. I then prepared a wash of Burnt Umber and French Ultramarine and drifted this in fairly strongly to the upper left and lower areas, taking care to prevent it covering the white paper below. I repeated this wash, a little more strongly, against the lower part of the sky, which had been allowed to dry slightly. These washes, as expected, dried out lighter in colour than they appeared when wet.

Before the sky and distance were completely dry, I tackled the large trees to the left with a strong wash of Ultramarine and Burnt Umber, applied with a no. 14 sable brush dragged on its side. This blended into the sky, suggesting a soft atmosphere. I repeated this wash for the nearest warm area of woodland to the right. The foreground field was given a wash of Ultramarine and Burnt Umber, mixing the colours on the paper, with the blue predominating to the right and the umber to the left. The washes were allowed to dry before I used the same two colours again, this time adding more blue than umber, for the cool tone of the distant trees on the right against the sky. I carried this colour over to the left to indicate the small, distant trees. Using a strong, dark tone of Burnt Umber with just a little Ultramarine, I drew in the branches and trunks of the main trees and the hedgerow below. With the same two colours but more of the blue on the right, I shaped up the foreground furrows, again dragging the brush across the paper to give texture.

You will by now have realized that I used very few colours for this painting – apart from the light area of sky, which I obtained with Light Red and Raw Sienna, only Burnt Umber and French Ultramarine were needed. This limited palette is very characteristic of much of my work – I tend to make use of warm and cool colours and tonal contrast, with the white of the paper playing an important part; in this case giving the highlight of the snow.

Figure 70 *Welsh Border.* 20 x 20 cm (8 x 12 in.), 480 gsm (220 lb) Richard de Bas Rough paper.

Georgian Bay

I found this subject on a bright day when visiting relatives in Canada. The dark trees bordering the lake made a strong contrast to the misty atmosphere over the water, which was frozen and covered with snow except for some nearer areas which were thawing. These open passages of water reflected the strong tones of the trees against the light of the snow. I made a quick tonal study in charcoal, which provided me with a basis upon which to work in the studio for my watercolour.

I washed in Monestial Blue for the sky from the top, blending in Burnt Sienna lower down and following with a soft wash of Monestial Blue for the lake. I left the white

of the paper for the light on the snow behind the trees. I repeated the blue and sienna wash for the nearer area of water. I next dealt with the dark group of trees on the left, with the same mixture applyied boldly with a no. 14 sable brush. I added more of the blue on the right for the more distant trees. Part of the sky was still damp, giving a soft edge to the trees and suggesting a misty atmosphere. I was careful to retain flecks of white paper for the snow shining through the lower part of the trees. I then drew in the trees on the right, using the same strong wash of Burnt Sienna and a little Monestial Blue. The lower sky wash was still damp which helped with the misty effect. I applied a darker wash over the near water area, with more blue, and while this was still wet drew in the darker reflections to right and left, resulting in soft edges. In the left foreground a touch of Burnt Sienna suggests the warm undergrowth and Monestial Blue with a little Burnt Umber drifted in gives a cooler effect. The near dark trees on left and right were drawn in strongly with Burnt Umber and a little Monestial Blue. I used the point of the brush for the finer lines, dragged on its side for the more textured areas of twigs. The two figures with their dog give human interest and a sense of scale. The Cadmium Red and Raw Sienna used for the figures add a useful colour note in an otherwise low-keyed picture. Their reflections were added while the water was still wet.

Figure 71 Sketch for *Georgian Bay*. 38 x 28 cm (15 x 11 in.), charcoal.

Figure 72 *Georgian Bay*. 39 x 28 cm (15 x 11 in.), 480 gsm (220 lb) Richard de Bas Rough paper.

HUBERT R·PHILLIPS

Demonstration: Worcestershire Winter

As you will see from the finished painting shown on page 96, there is an atmosphere of hushed stillness in the winter wood, especially under a fall of snow. At this time of year contrasts in the landscape are exaggerated with the bold, dark, angular shapes of the bare trees standing out against the snow and the sky. I try to capture the mood by first of all making a quick charcoal sketch which, together with a few jotted notes on colour, will enable me to complete a finished picture in the studio. Washes will not dry if I try to paint in the enclosed atmosphere of a wood.

Snow, stark white against grey, cool background. of sky and distance. Warm tints, Burnt Sienna etc. in near undergrowth. Silence and stillness, soft misty atmosphere

Figure 73 Sketch for *Worcestershire Winter*. 28 x 41 cm (11 x 16 in.), charcoal.

Stage 1

As the first step, I washed in Monestial Blue in the top left area of the sky, blending it into a delicate mix of Light Red and Raw Sienna on the right. I carried the wash down to where the snow begins behind the trees, leaving this as white paper.

Stage 2

Whilst the background of sky was still moist, I mixed Light Red and French Ultramarine and washed this in to indicate the shapes of the more distant trees. The warm area of sky to the right had dried out somewhat and this allowed me to suggest the texture of bare branches by dragging the brush (a no. 14 sable) on its side. I drifted in a little Burnt Sienna in the lower part of the right-hand wash and combined this colour with Monestial Blue below. I used the same blue along the track on the left.

Stage 3: The finished painting

I needed to be more specific in dealing with the trees, so I drew them in with the point of my brush, waiting until the previous washes were dry for crisper definition. Ultramarine and Burnt Umber were used for this, with a little more Burnt Umber for the near left-hand tree and Ultramarine predominating in the trees behind. I added Burnt Sienna to indicate the warm undergrowth colours to the right and left of the largest foreground tree. The figure was drawn in with Light Red and Burnt Sienna, with the head of the man and his dog in Ultramarine and Burnt Umber. Throughout the painting there was a constant need to retain areas of the white paper for the light snow.

Figure 74 *Worcestershire Winter*. Stage 3 (the finished painting), 26 x 33 cm (10½ x 14 in.), 480 gsm (220 lb) Richard de Bas Rough paper.

Figure 75 *Snow Showers.* 33 x 28 cm (13 x 19 in.).

Snow Showers

These dark snow showers were sweeping down across the sunlit cloud. Where the light broke through, it cast a glow over the snow-covered landscape. The distant mountain peaks were stark against the brooding horizon.

In my picture the dark tones of the distant woods create a sharp contrast against the light snow and provide a background to the small farm buildings, which give a useful feeling of scale. A simple foreground of pale blue shadows across the white snow leads the eye in to the distant landscape.

When painting snow scenes, it is important not to let the whiteness of the snow dominate. Ensure you leave enough uncovered details to create an interesting landscape where contrast between lights and darks is of the essence. Colour will come from the sky which is often what attracts me to a scene, with pale pastel-coloured clouds and delicate sunlight echoed in soft shadows and reflections.

CHAPTER 7
Distance and Space

The scale of elements in a painting also helps to create the correct feeling of distance and space. The dark, definite colour of the rocks in the foreground of these paintings of Tenerife stand out against the softer shades of the mountain in the distance and the small buildings at the foot of the slopes. When creating atmospheric perspective, it is usual to use dark, warm colours in the foreground and contrast this with cooler blues and greys in the background.

Tenerife 1
It was a pleasant experience to be able to sit on the beach in warm sunshine and paint this scene on a January morning. Mount Teide was a strong image in the distance on the right against the warm sky and this was balanced by the strong rocks in the foreground. The deep tones of the sea against the horizon contrasted with the white breakers. The figures on the rocks gave a sense of scale.

Tenerife 2
This was a softer, more atmospheric study than the one above. Mount Teide was softened a little by the mist of the day and the sunshine played on the distant buildings and sparkled on the sea.

Figure 76 *Tenerife 1.* 28 x 38 cm (11 x 15 in.).

Figure 77 *Tenerife 2.* 28 x 38 cm (11 x 15 in.).

Tenerife 3, Tenerife 4

These two studies were made looking out to sea. The light shone from a bright sky, sparkling on the water for which I used the white of the paper as highlights. The warm sands and deep-toned rocks were in strong contrast.

As the sky is reflected in the sea, other colours must be introduced into the picture with cliffs or rocks placed in the middle distance and foreground sand. Still pools left by the sea, in which rocks may be reflected as dark shapes, will help to give interest to the finished picture.

Figure 78 *Tenerife 3. 19 x 27 cm (7½ x 10½ in.).*

Painting by the sea when the view stretches over a large area is quite a challenge. The sun may be dazzling in which case it will be reflected in a large area of bright water. It is easier to paint from a shady or less windswept spot, perhaps with the cliffs behind you, rather than down near the water's edge. It is easy to end up with large expanses of sky and sea, which does not make a very captivating picture. An interesting sky with some movement and contrast will always be more successful than a completely cloudless one, while a boat or two will bring immediate interest to the sea. One or two figures on the beach will also act as a focal point.

Figure 79   *Tenerife 4*. 19 x 27 cm (7½ x 10½ in.).

September Landscape

Here we have an example of a picture in which I have attempted to deal with recession. The Cotswolds are familiar territory for me, being not far from my home and where I did some of my first painting direct from Nature. They are set on a plateau of rolling, undulating country, with open spaces giving prospects of distant low hills, or wolds, and are rather exposed to the elements. They provide a wonderful setting for the observance of distance and space – I stress the word 'observance' because before we can do anything about depicting a subject we must first observe intently.

In memory I take myself back to a fine, warm September afternoon with the kind of misty atmosphere often associated with early autumn. After exploring a bit, I found an attractive prospect across a cornfield. The crop had already been harvested but a few bales of straw had been left on the stubble, providing a spot of interest in an otherwise empty scene. Groups of trees grew at intervals, offering other points of interest.

Preliminary sketch

I took up my sketchbook and with a thick stick of charcoal set about exploring the composition of my subject, together with its tonal relationships. I like to use a piece of charcoal about 2.5 cm (1 in.) or so long, which I can apply flat on its side for blocking large areas or on its end for more precise drawing.

I first of all indicated the distant wolds with a soft touch about a third of the way up the paper. This left me a large area of paper in which to make full use of the sky, which contained some interesting formations, and would help in achieving the effect of recession. With the charcoal on its side and again using a soft touch, I applied it to large areas of the sky and rubbed it in well with my fingers to produce a soft grey tone. With the aid of a putty eraser, which is soft and tacky, I lifted out some of these areas to reveal the white of the paper and to suggest the light shapes of clouds.

With firm pressure, I established the dark group of trees to the left of the composition and balanced this with the smaller, more distant groups over to the right. I needed to move these in a little to bring them into the format of the picture – I often find the need to adjust my subject matter in this way in order to achieve a good composition. These tree groups provide a strong, dark tone which contrasted with the softer distance.

For the foreground cornfield I used the charcoal on its side for the near, textured area and on its end for the darker shapes of the straw bales. I now felt that I had explored the possibilities of my subject with regard to composition, tonal relationships, basic shapes of trees, cloud formation, etc.

I now had more confidence to take up my watercolours, knowing that my composition was sound and my notes truly related. This initial charcoal drawing gave me a good foundation before I could start to build a more comprehensive work in full colour with any hope of success.

Figure 80 *September Landscape, Cotswolds.* Charcoal sketch, 28 x 38 cm (11 x 15 in.).

Figure 81 *September Landscape, Cotswolds.* Stage 1

Stage 1

I first of all dealt with the sky as in a painting this sets the mood of the day, gives an indication of the weather, is a source of light and provides the background against which we need to judge the values of our nearer objects, in this case trees and distant hills. I worked from the light tones, covering large areas through the middle and finally the darks. I prepared large washes of colour on my palette so that I did not need to pause to mix more, which would have risked the washes already applied drying with hard edges in the meantime. I began by mixing Light Red and Raw Sienna for the light warm tones of the clouds, French Ultramarine and Burnt Umber for the grey, and Monestial Blue for the background sky. With my paper set on the drawing board at an angle of about 30° and using a no. 14 sable brush, I washed on the Light Red/Raw Sienna mixture for the light clouds to the top right and lower down by the horizon. I followed this with Monestial Blue to the upper left, allowing it to drift into the edges of the light clouds. These washes were applied to dry paper, allowing me to retain areas of pure white paper to act as highlights in the clouds. When the washes began to dry slightly, I applied the Ultramarine/Burnt Umber mixture to the darker areas of cloud. These washes did not blend in as freely as the first because by now the paper was slightly drying

Stage 2

out, giving more definite shapes although still with soft edges. Before the sky was dry, I quickly repeated the Light Red/Raw Sienna wash into the cornfield area below, carrying it over the entire passage and adding rather more Raw Sienna, allowing it to mix on the paper. The paper was now entirely covered with these light washes except for the untouched areas in the sky. I made use of the Rough surface of the paper by swiftly dragging the brush (a no. 14 sable) across when I applied the sky washes, thus suggesting broken light clouds. Before this wash dried I added the Ultramarine/Burnt Umber mixture to the distant parts of the landscape. This blended in, leaving soft edges

to indicate the misty hills. When this was nearly dry I suggested the shapes of small groups of tree, using the same mixture but a little darker than before.

Stage 2

I now took a breather while the washes dried out, knowing that when I returned I should see the work with a fresh eye. Feeling the need to stretch my legs after sitting for so long, I became aware of an alternative composition which I sketched in charcoal. Together with the experience gained from painting the first picture, this enabled me to produce another version of this intriguing subject in the studio.

I began painting again by mixing a dark green with Monestial Blue and Raw Sienna and washed this in for each tree group. I applied a mid-tone of Burnt Umber with a little Ultramarine over the cornfield, using quick strokes of the brush to capture the rough surface of the stubble. I returned to the near trees with a strong mixture of Burnt Sienna and Monestial Blue, applied boldly to draw in the dark shapes of the trees and their shadows. I used a lighter version of this mixture for the right-hand group and Burnt Umber and Ultramarine for the shadowed area behind. A weaker tone of this mixture, with more Burnt Umber, suggested the straw and the darker tones on the stubble.

The finished painting

Before deciding whether the picture was finished I waited to enclose it in a mount. It can be fatal to continue working for too long on a painting on the spot. Often when you can view the work away from the subject you are better able to judge its worth.

I decided that, although it falls short of what I would have liked, there was little that I could do to improve it without losing its freshness. I felt I had managed to capture something at least of the mood, atmosphere and space. The contrast in tone of the darks of the trees against the soft misty distances and the warm colours of the larger trees, corn stubble and bales against the cooler distant landscape play an important part in this. Including a large area of sky and the trees in the middle distance diminishing in scale both help with the feeling of space.

Figure 82 *September Landscape, Cotswolds.* 29 x 39 cm (11½ x 15½ in.)

CHAPTER 8
Details and Skies

It is quite apparent from my pictures that I do not work in great detail. I find that a broad treatment can carry more conviction and I am in sympathy with that approach. Detail is, of course, relative to the subject – we obviously see much more in the foreground than in the distance – so in order to attract the eye to focus in that area I need to keep the foreground simple, allowing the eye to pass over it and into the picture.

In many of my paintings the sky plays a major role, often occupying most of the space compared to the landscape below. Skies convey weather and atmosphere, which set the mood for a painting, and they are endlessly fascinating to paint in their own right.

In this chapter I have chosen to include paintings where the emphasis is on the sky and on specific details such as trees, shadows, the effects of weather and shapes of hills and mountains. I had no difficulty in finding plenty of examples as I am consistently drawn to scenes with dramatic skies and distant hills. The technique of capturing recession is a constant challenge and I am always trying to improve my skills in this area. I cannot urge the student enough to do the same.

Figure 83 *Light over the Moelwyns.* 41 x 56 cm (16 x 22 in.).

Light over the Moelwyns

In this picture I have simplified the foreground with a cloud shadow, making use of the Rough texture of the paper. The attention is given to the sunlit passage and the impressive contours of the Moelwyn Mountains against the sky. The sunlight clouds and those which are darker are in keeping with the sunlight and shadow on the landscape below.

When the main interest of a painting is in the beauty or drama of the sky, it would be foolish to distract the viewer by painting foreground details. The excitement of ever-changing cloud shapes and patterns of light should be allowed to speak for itself. Here the dark cloud shadow over the foreground contrast with the sunshine from above creating a dynamic picture without the need for painstaking foreground detail.

Trees against the Light

This is a study of the texture and detail of
dark trees in silhouette against a sunlit
background. I made use of the Rough surface
of the paper, dragging the brush on its side
for the dark passages of foliage and using the
point for the trunks and branches. I made no
attempt at composition, my main concerns
were the dark, textured trees against the light
and the sky and the cool distance beyond.

Figure 84 *Trees against the Light*. 37 x 33 cm (14½ x 13 in.).

Autumn Trees

The main interest here is in the foreground area – the dark trees against the sky and the hedgerows on each side. I used the Rough surface of the paper to capture the detail of the trees, dragging a large brush on its side to get the texture of leaves and twigs, and using the point of the brush for the branches. The dark, warm tones of the foreground contrast with the cooler distance and the rutted track leads in through the gap in the hedgerow. Details such as telegraph posts, broken or steady gates and small bridges need careful study and drawing practice. The pattern of knots on trees, the way branches meet the central trunk, how fallen branches lie in woodland areas – all these subjects depend on the realistic depiction of texture, shape and proportion. Don't forget to include the correct details of country crafted objects. Bridges, for instance, must have a central keystone – no bridge or gate arch can exist without this.

Figure 85 *Autumn Trees*. 28 x 39 cm (11½ x 15½ in.).

A Sutherland Farm

It was the dramatic effect in the sky which gave interest to this picture, with the large cloud on the left sweeping down to soften the contours of the distant mountains. The dark, cool tones of the lower hills made a useful foil for the farm buildings, which stood out against them. The burn and rocks in the foreground are simply treated, leading the eye across the sunlit middle distance to the farm buildings, which give scale and interest.

Menai Straits

It was again the dominating sky which gave impact to this subject. The rainclouds softened the distant mountains on the left and the light broke through and reflected in the water of the Straits. The boats to the left break up that area of shadow with their light masts and give scale and interest.

Isle of Man

It was a lovely day of moving cloud, with the sun breaking through to create a sparkling light over the distant line of the sea below the darker headland. The warm seaweed-covered rocks in the foreground and the deep blue of the sea provide a tonal base to the composition. The foreground was treated very broadly.

Figure 86 *Sutherland Farm*. 34 x 30 cm (13½ x 12 in.).

Figure 87 *Menai Straits.* 28 x 38 cm (11 x 15 in.).

Figure 88 *Isle of Man.* 28 x 38 cm (11 x 15 in.).

Figure 89 *A Calm Evening.* 29 x 42 cm (11½ x 16½ in.), charcoal.

A Calm Evening

This piece has simple and dramatic contours, the wide river bordered by banks with the steep right-hand one casting a deep shadow in the river. The textured marks of the charcoal convey the magical quality of the gentle light and evening atmosphere.

View from Sanna Bay

This was a lovely, serene evening. The warm clouds parted to allow the departing sun to light up the band of sea below the distant islands. The sandy shore and headlands of the foreground are simply treated in keeping with the lovely evening light.

View on Skye

This was towards evening, with rain showers softening the distant mountains of mainland Scotland and the sun lighting up the waters of the Sound of Sleat. The trees in the left foreground gave a useful warm, dark area, balanced by the deep tones of the wooded slopes to the right. I kept the whole foreground area simple in treatment and low in key, to give value to the light of the sky and its reflection in the water.

Figure 90 *View from Sanna Bay.* 19 x 28 cm (7½ x 11 in.).

Figure 91 *View on Skye.* 28 x 39 cm (11 x 15½ in.).

Rain Showers

The rain showers breaking the line of the distant mountains gave me the main subject matter for this picture. The sun broke through, flooding the middle distance and farm buildings with a theatrical light, contrasted with the darker tones of the lower mountains behind and the shadowed foreground. This was a broadly treated subject, with the main detail and interest focused on the middle distance beyond a simple foreground.

This picture is another instance of how a scene breaks down into distance, middle distance and foreground. Had the sun not decided to shine on the farm buildings in the centre of the picture as I watched, my interpretation of the view might have been quite different.

Figure 92 *Rain Showers*. 34 x 43 cm (13½ x 17 in.).

Figure 93 *Summer Tree.* 38 x 27 cm (15 x 10½ in.).

Figure 94 *Clearing after Rain.* 25 x 33 cm (10 x 13 in), Whatman tinted paper

Summer Tree

This is a study of a tree in the full foliage of high summer. I have attempted to convey the basic structure of the supporting trunk and branches, using the fine point of my rigger brush after broadly washing in the main areas. The figure and dog on the right and the gate and fencing on the left were captured in the same way.

Clearing after Rain

I used a sheet of old sand-coloured Whatman paper, which imparted a lovely warm glow to this study. It was a day of swiftly moving clouds, with the sun breaking through in places throwing parts of the landscape into shadow and others into strong light.

The paper is untouched by washes in parts of the sky, particularly above the tallest tree to the left, and reveals its natural colour.

I worked this study in a very wet state, bringing the stormclouds down on the right over the distant hills while retaining the light sky behind the tallest tree on the left as a contrast.

Figure 95 *Thorn Tree*. 38 x 25 cm (15 x 10 in.).

Thorn Tree

I was attracted to this old thorn tree struggling for existence against the blast of countless winters and the heat of many summers on the slopes of Glencoe. It made an interesting study with its dark shapes against the snow-capped peaks beyond.

Figure 96 *Stormy Sky*. 29 x 38 cm (11½ x 15 in.), charcoal. The pointed steeple provides a static form and scale against the moving clouds with the light breaking through.

Stormy Sky

A dramatic sky such as this is always inspiring. Such exciting lighting conditions can come about with little warning, so I always keep a pad in the car together with drawing materials to sketch the shape of the clouds quickly. The key to this scene is a sense of movement and the impressive grandeur and power of nature. Try to practise cloud painting, keeping your paper damp to express their soft diffused edges.

Having eventually (usually at home in my studio) finished a sky to my satisfaction, I am ready to tackle the foreground. A steeple or church tower is always a bonus when painting landscapes. It will often become the focal point as it rises into the lower clouds.

CONCLUSION

For many years I have had the pleasure of working with people motivated by the sheer joy of painting. What better pursuit can there be than to respond in a creative way to the beauties we see around us, attempting to capture them and share them with others? These painters may not claim to have reached the highest standards of technique, but they have that quality of sincerity and integrity in their work which is sadly lacking in much that is produced in the name of art today.

You may be moved by the play of light and shade over a landscape, the pounding of a rough sea on a rocky shore or the tranquil reflections of evening light on a beach at low tide. We all have our differing tastes and convictions, to which we should hold fast – 'To thine own self be true.'

Above all we must have patience with ourselves. I am still learning new techniques in my work, finding different ways of looking at and interpreting the landscape on paper and I still enjoy the excitement of seeing a picture develop on my easel. I encourage all who enjoy painting to keep at it – never give up and try not to get too disheartened when things do not go so well. There is always another sheet of paper waiting for your next attempt and sometimes when you least expect it you will produce something truly rewarding.

LIST OF SUPPLIERS

UK

Winsor & Newton
51-2 Rathbone Place
London
W1P 1AB

Caran d'Ache
  Jakar International Ltd
Hillside House
2–6 Friern Park
London
N12 9BX

East London Graphics
86–99 Upton Lane
London
E7 8LQ

London Graphic Centre
107–115 Long Acre
London
WC2

UDO City
69–85 Old Street
London
EC1V 9HX

Cornelissens
105 Great Russell Street
London
WC1B 3RY

Artworks
28 Spruce Drive
Paddock Wood
Lightwater
Surrey
GU18 5YX

Pullingers Stationers
109 West Street
Farnham
Surrey
GU9 7HH

Hearn & Scott
10 Bridge Street
Andover
Hampshire
SP10 1BH

R S Frames
4 Broomfield Road
Sunbury-on-Thames
Middlesex
TW16 6SW

Broad Canvas
20 Broad Street
Oxford
OX1 3AS

Daler-Rowney
PO Box 10
Bracknell
Berkshire
RG12 8ST

Gemini Craft Supplies
14 Shakespeare Street
Newcastle upon Tyne
Tyne & Wear
NE1 6AQ

James Dinsdale Ltd
22–4 King Charles Street
Leeds
LS1 6LT

Merseyside Framing
& Arts Ltd
62–4 Wavertree Road
Liverpool
L7 1PH

John E Wright & Co
15 Brick Street
Derby
DE1 1DU

Everyman
13 Cannon Street
Birmingham
G2 5EN

Rod Waspe
11–13 Bank Street
Rugby
CV21 2QE

Colemans
84 High Street
Huntingdon
Cambs
PE18 6DP

Windsor Gallery
167 London Road South
Lowestoft
Suffolk
NR33 0DR

Doodles
61 High Street
Newport Pagnell
Bucks
MK16 8AT

Framework
63 Pembroke Centre
Cheney Manor
Swindon
Wiltshire
SN2 2PQ

Dicketts
6 High Street
Glastonbury
Somerset
BA6 9DU

Mair & Son
46 The Strand
Exmouth
Devon
EX8 1AL

CJ Graphic Supplies Ltd
32 Bond Street
Brighton
Sussex
BN1 1RQ

Forget-Me-Not
70 Upper James Street
Newport
Isle of Wight
PO30 1LQ

Elsa Frisher
9 St Peter's Square
Ruthin
Clwyd
LL15 1DH

Inkspot
1–2 Upper Clifton Street
Cardiff
South Glamorgan
CF2 3JB

Alexander's Art Shop
58 South Clerk Street
Edinburgh
EH8 9PS

Burns & Harris
163–165 Overgate
Dundee
DD1 1QF

The EDCO Shop
47–49 Queen Street
Belfast
BT1 6HP

Millers Ltd
11–15 Clarendon Place
St George's Cross
Glasgow
G20 7PZ

USA

Aiko's Art Materials
 Import
3347 N. Clark Street
Chicago
Illinois 60657

Badger Air-Brush Company
9128 West Belmont Ave
Franklin Park
Illinois 60131

Fletcher-Lee & Co.
PO Box 007
Elk Grove Village
Illinois 60009

Printmakers Machine Co.
PO Box 71
Villa Park
Illinois 60181

Pearl Paint Company
307 Canal Street
New York 10013

New York Central
 Art Supply
62 3rd Avenue
New York 10003

Artist's Connection
20 Constance Ct
PO Box 13007
Hauppauge
New York 11788

Winsor & Newton
PO Box 1396
Piscataway
New Jersey 08855

The Italian Art Store
84 Maple Avenue
Morristown
New Jersey 07960

Art Supply Warehouse
360 Main Avenue
Norwalk
Connecticut 06851

The Artist's Club
5750 NE Hassalo Street
Portland
Oregon 97213

Texas Art Supply
2001 Montrose Boulevard
Houston
Texas 77006

Sax Arts and Crafts
PO Box 51710
New Berlin
Wisconsin 53151

Perma Colour
226 E Tremont
Charlotte
North Carolina 28203

Co-op Artists' Materials
PO Box 53097
Atlanta
Georgia 30355

Chroma Acrylics Inc.
205 Bucky Drive
Lititz
Pittsburgh 17543

Conrad Machine Co.
1525 S. Warner
Whitehall
Michigan 49461

HK Holbein Inc.
PO Box 555
Williston
VT 05495

Ziegler
PO Box 50037
Tulsa
Oklahoma 74150

Art Express
1561 Broad River Road
Columbia
SC 29210

Pentel of America Ltd
2805 Columbia Street
Torrance
California 90503

Napa Valley Art Store
1041 Lincoln Avenue
Napa
California 94558

INDEX

Note that page references in *italics* refer to illustrations